JOHN CHAMBERLAIN

JOHN CHAMBERLAIN

RECENT SCULPTURE OCTOBER 21–DECEMBER 3, 2005

PACEWILDENSTEIN
545 WEST 22ND STREET NEW YORK NY 10001

THE SCULPTURE OF JOHN CHAMBERLAIN: AN UGLY BEAUTY

by Irving Sandler

In 1960, I published an article surveying Assemblage—the first to my knowledge—that featured John Chamberlain's construction-sculptures, among other works. Assemblage then was still commonly known as Neo-Dada, the new anti-art, because it was composed of rubbishy materials.[1] To be sure, the detritus looked raw and "unfinished," but so did Jackson Pollock's impetuous "drip" and Willem de Kooning's slashed and scraped painterly drawing—and they were accepted and esteemed. In retrospect, it is difficult to fathom why at that time the New York School, the international center of the avant-garde, found junk materials beyond the pale of art. After all, what made art avant-garde was its challenge to conventional taste, but the line was drawn at discarded materials, particularly those which seemed "untransformed," and notably Chamberlain's crushed and crumpled auto parts.

In my 1960 essay, I alluded to the resemblance of Chamberlain's sculpture to automobile detritus. But I was quick to stress the formal attributes of the work—and its formal intelligence. "Design is of primary significance in the constructions of Chamberlain. Not only does he cut scrap metal to desired forms but he carefully balances their battered colors. [The] adjustment of colors and their invented forms seem to predominate over the images of wreckage that his works evoke."[2]

Chamberlain himself denied any relation of his materials to the role of the automobile in American life: "I wasn't interested in the car parts *per se*. I was interested in either the color or the shape. . . . Just the sheet metal. It already had a coat of paint on it, and some of it was formed."[3] Moreover, Chamberlain found discarded car parts—his "art supplies" or "palette," as he quipped—to his liking because they were inexpensive or free, readily available in ubiquitous automobile graveyards, malleable, and brand-new in art.

Brian O'Doherty best summed up how the recycled scrap metal functions in Chamberlain's sculptures. He wrote, "a common material with a pre-formed mythic content shakes off its origins through formal transformations, even though the result makes a mockery of formalism."[4] And in its unpolished look, Chamberlain's "bulldozer drapery" makes a mockery of the slickness of new cars and their glitzy advertisements.

Central to the formal transformations of which O'Doherty wrote is Chamberlain's masterful use of automobile lacquer and enamel colors (and after 1961 pigments he sprayed and painted to expand his range of colors and make it more individual). Chamberlain was one of only two sculptors to use color boldly in the late 1950s (the other was George Sugarman), and his readymade automobile colors constituted an unprecedented palette in art. We forget today how rare, problematic, and risky the introduction of color in sculpture was in the late fifties and early sixties, particularly commercial colors associated with popular culture. America's most powerful critic at the time, Clement Greenberg, intent on "purifying" the various art mediums, insisted that color was an attribute of painting and denied that it had any role in sculpture. Chamberlain, however, wasn't listening. In retrospect, the controversy seems trivial, but it didn't then.

The way in which Chamberlain's auto body parts call attention to their sources in the world and play a decisive formal role in his constructions seems contradictory. But it points to his predilection for synthesizing antitheses, among them painting and sculpture, tradition and innovation, abstraction and figuration, and Abstract Expressionism and Pop and Minimal Art. Indeed, Chamberlain's juggling of complex visual dialectics in his sculpture is the key to its depth and dimension.

The synthesis of painting and sculpture is central to Chamberlain's work. His early metal constructions were influenced by David Smith's works, but in the late 1950s, they increasingly alluded to de Kooning's Gesture or Action Painting. As Chamberlain remarked, it was the tendency with which he felt "intuitively in tune."[5] He was taken with the roughness, muscularity, and energy of de Kooning's painting and the ambiguity of its shifting and interpenetrating open planes. These gave Chamberlain permission to use smashed car parts that seemed to be in constant motion. But he was not satisfied with

Gesture Painting's two-dimensions, and he translated its flat forms into bulky and swelling volumes, both in reliefs and in-the-round sculptures. In the process, Chamberlain transformed Gesture Painting and achieved an original style.

Above all, Chamberlain was influenced by the improvisational approach of Gesture Painting. As he said, "you have to go with the process. There's no formula. . . . I just run on intuition and use that as a general mediator among emotion and sexuality and drive. . . . All of a sudden, at some point, there's nothing else to do."[6] He also added that the main activity for him as an artist was "to find out what you don't know. To start someplace that's curious to you and delve into it in a common way and come out with an uncommon satisfaction . . . that is very satisfying to your nervous system."[7] Consequently, improvisation enabled Chamberlain to follow his feelings in piecing together auto body parts until their relationships were felt, or as he put it, each "*fits*, it's just the right thing at the right moment."[8] The sculpture that his trial and error process yields often has the look of unrestrained impulsiveness, but it is painstakingly judged. Every spontaneous move is weighed both for its felt and formal rightness. Chamberlain once titled a piece *Cautious Maniac*, a fitting description of the artist in action.[9]

The physicality, dynamism, and rawness of Chamberlain's constructions, which were anticipated by de Kooning's and Kline's Gesture Painting, have often been viewed as distinctively American. De Kooning, for example, denigrated contemporary French artists because they had a certain "touch" that makes their works look like "'finished' paintings," a touch he was glad not to have.[10] Chamberlain emulated this energy and crudeness in his work, but in his unique robust manner. Physically brawny, his natural body language led him to engage in "squeezing and hugging," as he put it.[11] Chamberlain's sculpture recalls the words of Ralph Waldo Emerson celebrating the "rough and ready style" of Americans, "the coarse energy of the 'bruisers' [who] have the good nature of strength and courage. [They] are usually frank and direct, and above falsehood."[12]

At the same time that Chamberlain's construction is crude, it is also beautiful in the best sense of that old-fashioned word. His obvious delight in the manipulation of his materials is manifest in his work. He applies lyrical colors—among them polka-dotted or peppermint-striped Kandy Kolors that risk being "pretty"—to exactly shaped metal components as foils or as camouflage for the rawness of his scarred, dented, and corroded metal parts. The contrast avoids the merely decorative and gives rise to an "Ugly Beauty," as Thelonious Monk titled one of his jazz pieces.[13]

Chamberlain's sculpture has often been coupled with that of Mark di Suvero, because the works of both artists were recognized at the moment when Gesture Painting had become an accepted, indeed, established style. To some it appeared to be overworked and if not yet academic, then on the verge. Welded construction, the then-current sculptural counterpart of Gesture Painting, was equally well established. If both had become an outworn tradition, it was nevertheless a tradition congenial to Chamberlain and di Suvero. Their aim, in part, became to reanimate construction sculpture, to make it truly contemporary. They succeeded by audaciously introducing found and prefabricated materials of city or industrial origin into their works, making them big, and in the case of Chamberlain, by making the components voluminous and using an automobile lacquer and enamel palette.

In the 1960s, Gesture Painting was challenged by Pop Art and Minimal Art, tendencies that were clearly antithetical to it. The relationship of Chamberlain's construction to these new movements was ambiguous. While his work remained in the ambit of Abstract Expressionism, it was linked by art writers to Pop Art because its incorporation of car parts appeared to refer to the automobile as the exemplary consumer icon. However, as an abstract artist Chamberlain made no direct reference to consumerism, as the pop realists Roy Lichtenstein and Andy Warhol did. With an eye to Minimal Art, Chamberlain introduced modularity and the unitary shape in a number of his works, including such later ones as *Thicket* (1997; plate 13) and *Neptune's Cap* (2005; plate 11). However, unlike Minimal Art, Chamberlain's process was improvisational, poles apart from the Minimalists' pre-conceptual approach. He became a friend of a number of Minimalist artists, but as Klaus Kertess observed, he was "the pagan friend of the monastic order."[14] It is significant that Chamberlain developed his sculptural style before the emergence of either Pop Art or Minimal Art. However, his work has always had the openness to absorb or incorporate new dialectics, as if it were in its nature to do so.

* * *

Almost from the start of Chamberlain's use of polychromed auto body parts, he found his sculptural vocabulary, a vocabulary sufficiently rich and open to enable him to create an extraordinarily varied body of sculpture.[15] Increasingly he has added paint to his pieces, in a staggering variety of multicolored airbrushed, stenciled, graffitied, and freehand painted brushmarks, sprays, pours, images, and patterns (with a nod to Pattern and Decoration Painting). In general, Chamberlain has worked in two divergent ways, which correspond to two of the main tendencies within Gesture Painting: a crude, aggressive, compacted "expressionism" reminiscent of de Kooning's painting, on the one hand and, on the other, a lyrical, field "impressionism" associated with Pollock's painting.

Sphinx (2004; plate 9) is in the "expressionist" vein. Tall, rising to just under 8 feet, it is composed of packed, scruffy, and bruised white and chrome auto parts. Chamberlain once said that his vertical pieces call to mind Rodin's *Balzac*.[16] *Sphinx* certainly does; it has a similar backward lean, but that can also be read as a strut.

In another direction, *Thicket* is composed of a series of five multicolored, hedge-like, rectangular shapes with spatial corridors between them that form a large cubic complex. The upper part of each "hedge" is a field of tangled ribbony forms that sits on a low complex of compacted, larger, crumpled rectangles, which suggests a sculptural base. Raw signs of mangled auto parts are played down. The work points up the polarities between pictorial flatness and sculptural mass. The "hedges" evoke Pollock's poured all-over painting. In their modular arrangement, they form a Minimal-like sculpture.

Both *Roots* (2003; plate 12) and *Neptune's Cap* are large, roughly cubic volumes that also refer to Minimalism. *Roots* is formed of two cubic elements, placed one on top the other. The upper cube is made up of sumptuously polychromed broad ribbons whose ebullience is countered by jangled elements, many of which are chrome, in the lower section. In contrast, *Neptune's Cap* is an all-chrome piece whose upper section, consisting of a mesh of interwoven, spiral linear components, sits on a lower section, composed of broader ribbons.

A number of vertical abstract constructions, titled *Spectators* (2005; plates 1–8), evoke standing personages. Viewed as figures, each has its own personality, which is revealed in its gesture. The subjects are often witty or comical, as are their titles. SGT. *Clappingstone* (plate 6) has elegant chrome shoes and tips his "hat" or salutes the viewer, while *Wanda Wedgie* (plate 7) waves seductively, and *Mrs. Swayed Schwooz* (plate 1) flings her parts out-of-control.

* * *

Given the complexity of Chamberlain's dialectics and the openness of his improvisational process, the diversity of his sculptures comes as no surprise. What distinguishes them all is their originality, inventiveness, and masterliness or, as Chamberlain put it, "it's all in the fit."[17]

Endnotes

1. "The Art of Assemblage," curated by William C. Seitz at The Museum of Modern Art in 1961, emphasized the aesthetic dimension in what had been known as Neo-Dada and led to the general use of the label Assemblage.
2. Irving Sandler, "Ash Can Revisited: A New York Letter," *Art International* (October 25, 1960), pp. 28, 30.
3. Julie Sylvester, "Auto/Bio: Conversations with John Chamberlain," in *John Chamberlain/New Sculpture*, exh. cat. (New York: Pace Gallery, 1991), pp. 11-12.
4. Brian O'Doherty, "Chamberlain: Projective Sculpture," in *John Chamberlain: Recent Sculpture*, exh. cat. (New York: PaceWildenstein, 1994), p. 8.
5. Sylvester, "Auto/Bio," p. 10.
6. Ibid., p. 16.
7. Ibid., p. 7.
8. Ibid.
9. David Anfam, "Chamberlain's Gambit: 'Cautious Maniac,'" in *John Chamberlain: Sculpture 1988–2001*, exh. cat. (London: Waddington Galleries, 2002), p. 5.
10. Willem de Kooning, quoted in Robert Goodnough, ed., "Artists' Sessions at Studio 35 (1950), in *Modern Artists in America* (New York: Wittenborn Schultz, 1951), p. 13.
11. Anfam, "Chamberlain's Gambit," p. 6.
12. Ralph Waldo Emerson, quoted in Harold Bloom, "The Sage of Concord," *The Guardian Review*, May 24, 2003, pp. 4-5.
13. Ken Johnson, in "Of Industry & Intuition," *Art in America* (April 1991), p. 134, called attention to the "oppositional tensions" in Chamberlain's work, among them "angry/playful; crude elegant; ugly/beautiful; brutal/delicate; [and] chaotic/harmonious."
14. Klaus Kertess, "Color in the Round and Then Some: John Chamberlain's Work, 1954-1985," in Julie Sylvester, *John Chamberlain: A Catalogue Raisonné of the Sculpture, 1954-1985* (Los Angeles: The Museum of Contemporary Art, 1986), p. 34.
15. From roughly 1967 to 1974 Chamberlain worked primarily in non-metal mediums, such as Plexiglas, foam rubber, latex, metal foil, and paper bags.
16. Henry Geldzahler, "Interview with John Chamberlain," in *John Chamberlain: Recent Work*, exh. cat. (New York: Pace Gallery, 1992), n.p.
17. Sylvester, "Auto/Bio," p. 12.

1. Mrs. Swayed Schwooz, 2005

painted and chromed steel
84 ½ x 74 ¾ x 41"

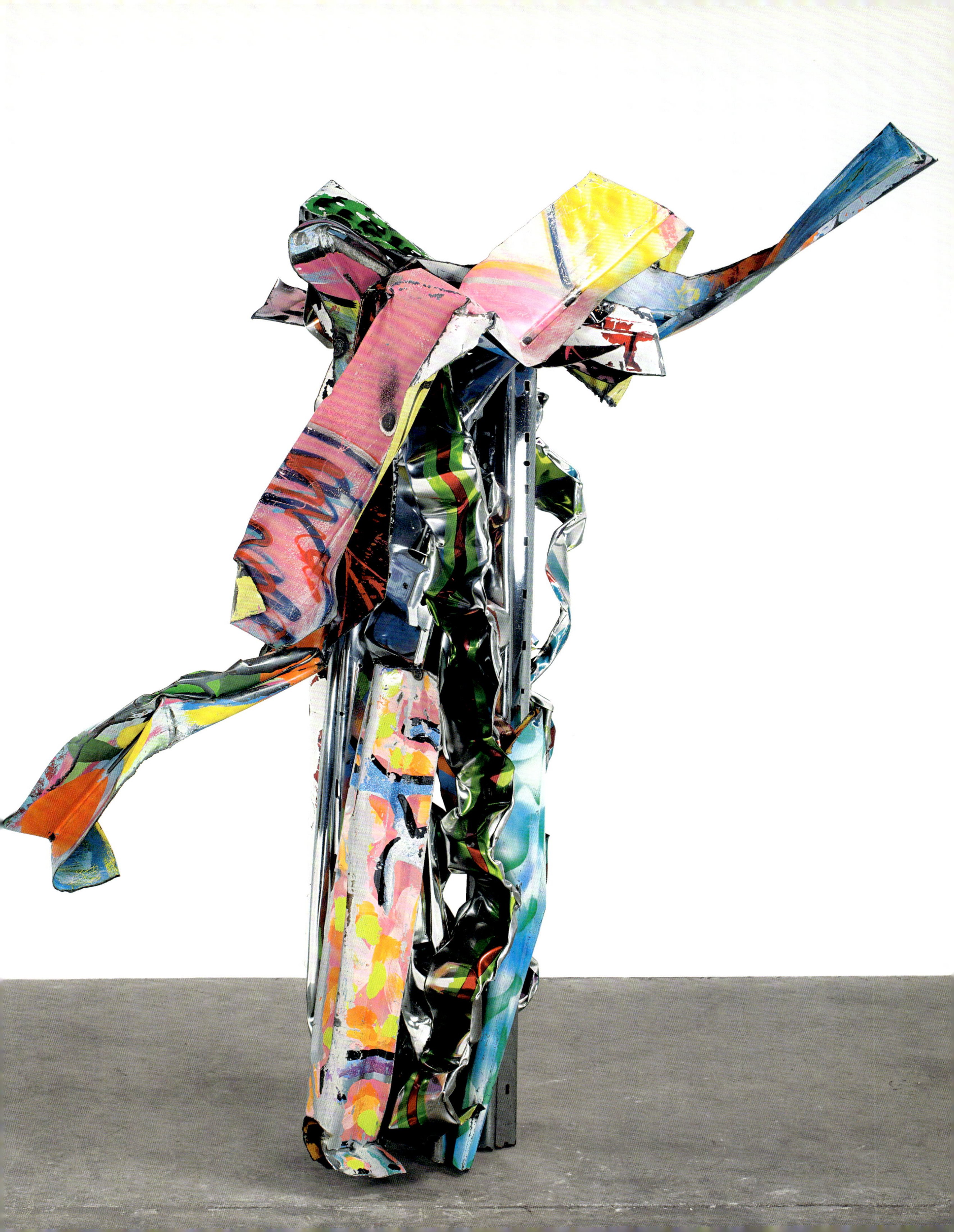

2. Madam ZooZoo, 2005

painted and chromed steel
80 x 25 x 22"

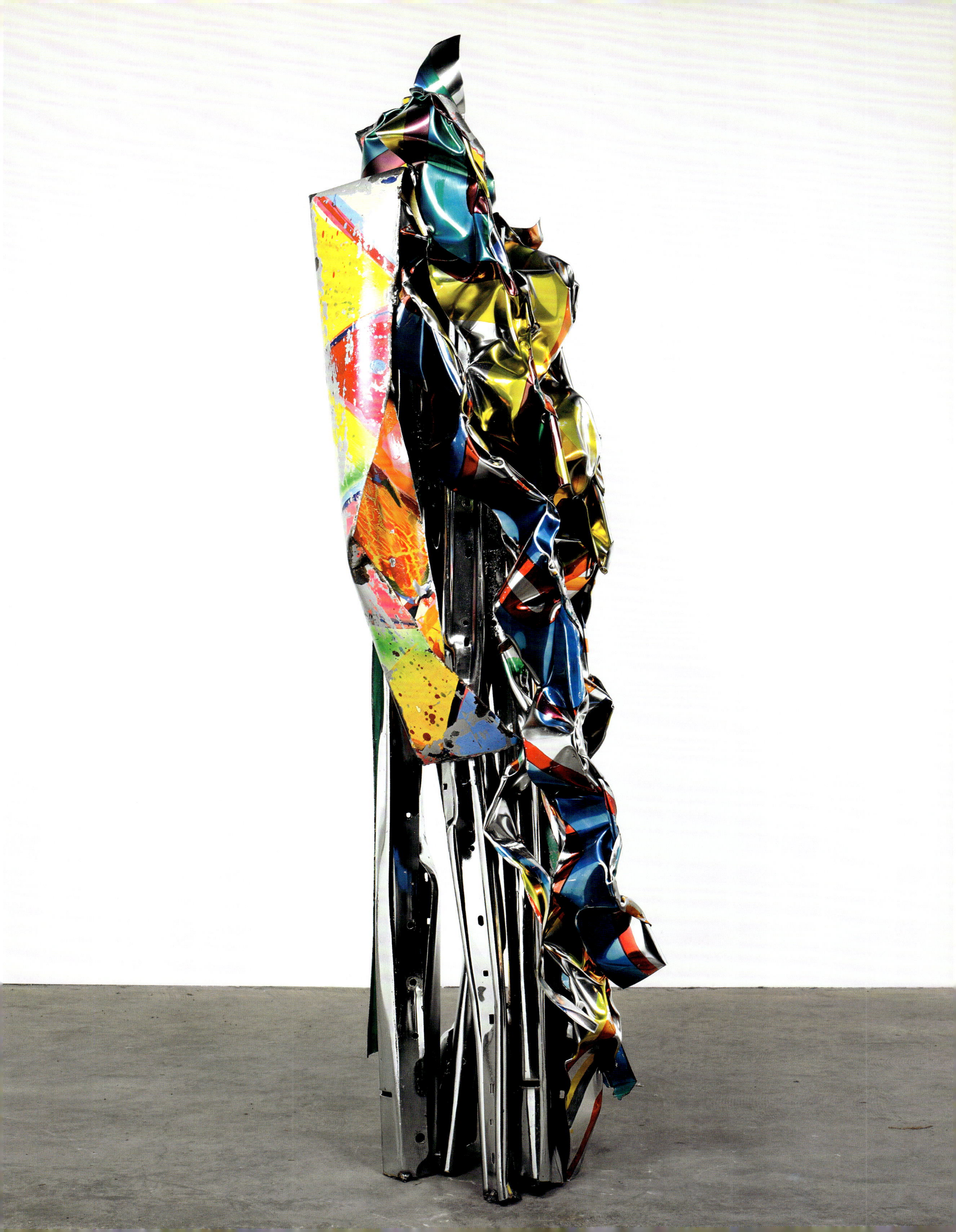

3. Mr. Mumblecrust, 2005

painted and chromed steel
74 ½ x 44 x 39 ¼"

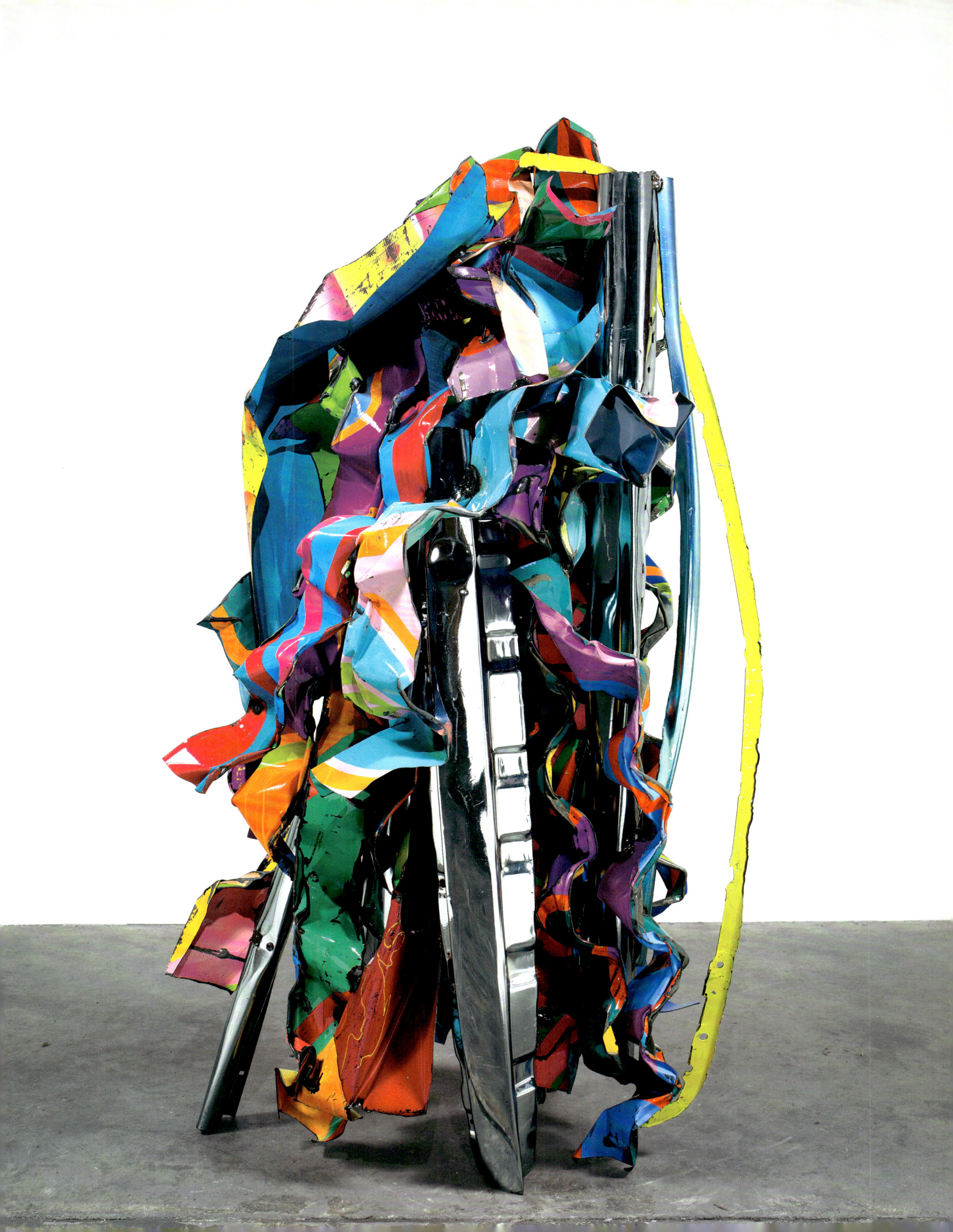

4. Rocket Ralph, 2005

painted and chromed steel
75 x 26 x 22"

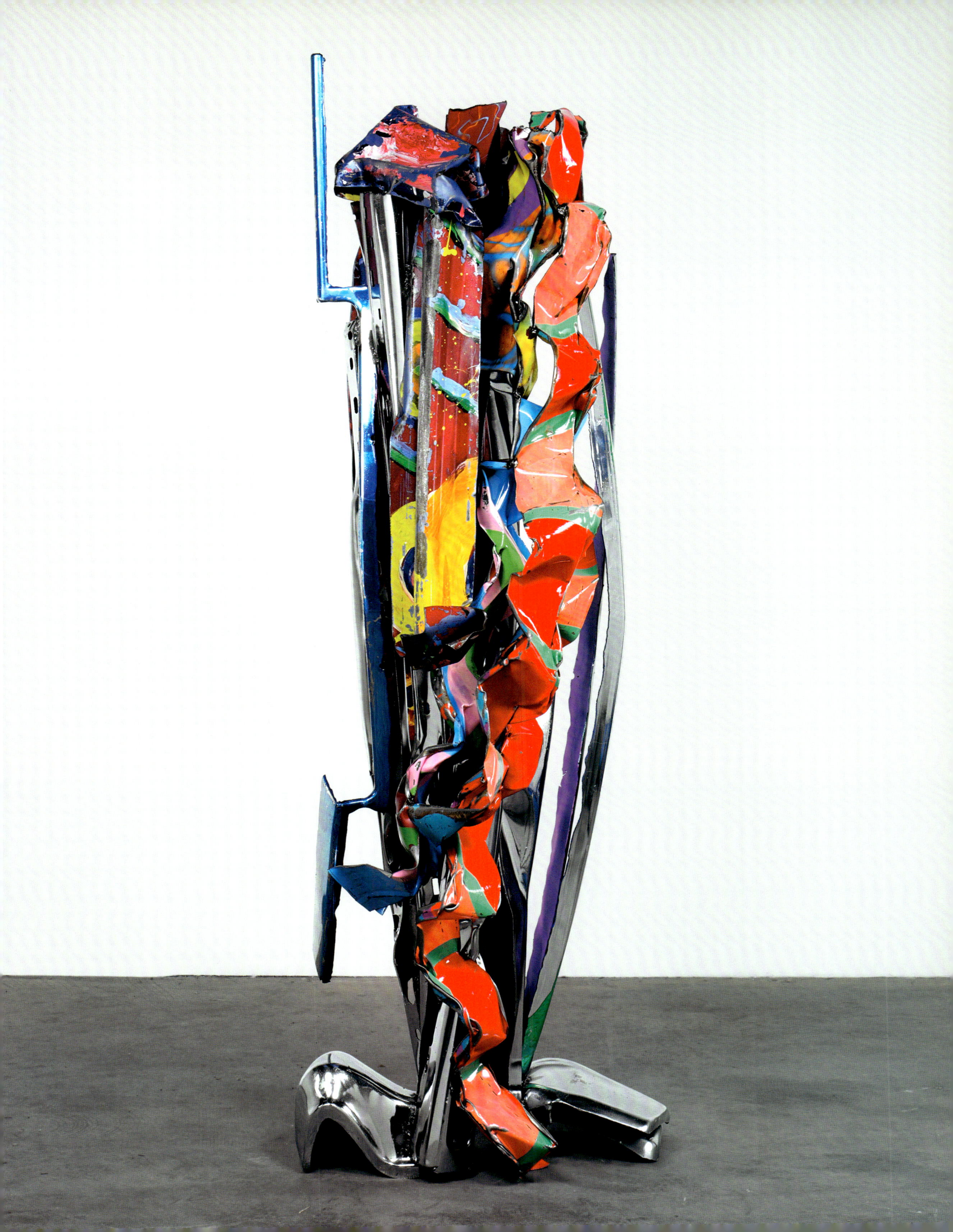

5. Ms. Trixie Friganza, 2005

painted and chromed steel
76 x 32 ¾ x 23 ½"

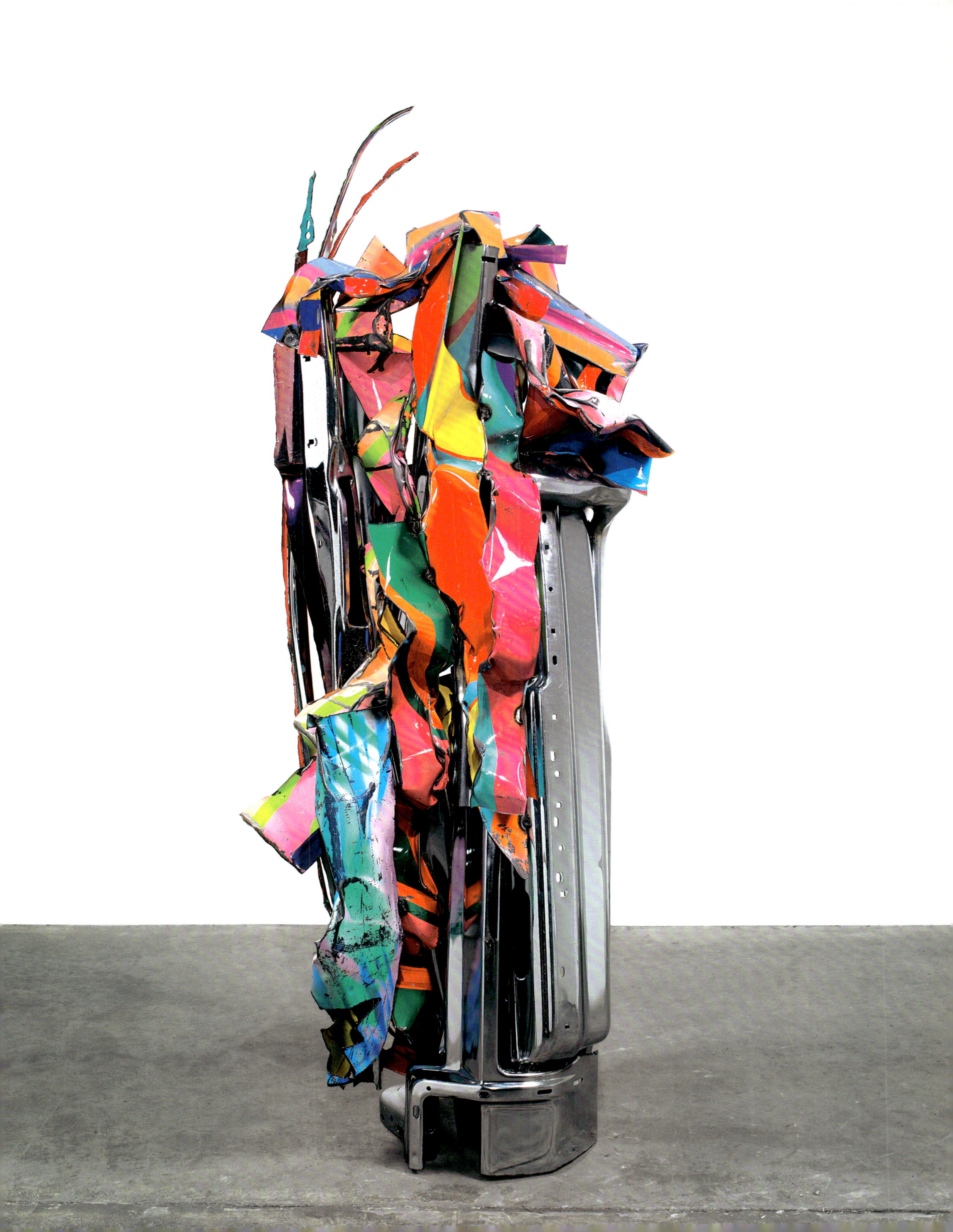

6. **SGT. Clappingstone**, 2005

painted and chromed steel
71 ½ x 26 x 23"

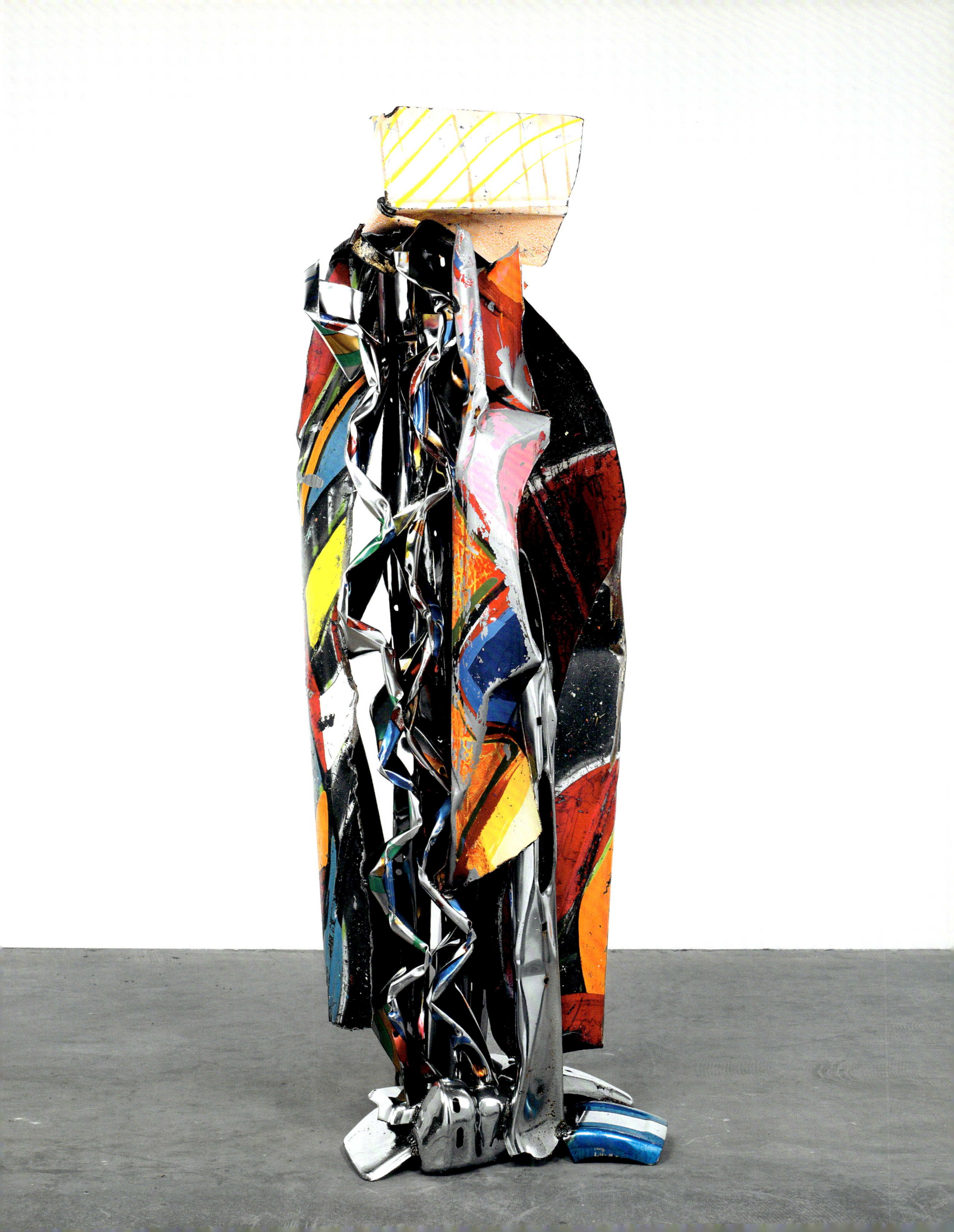

7. **Wanda Wedgie**, 2005

painted and chromed steel
77 ¾ x 38 ½ x 27"

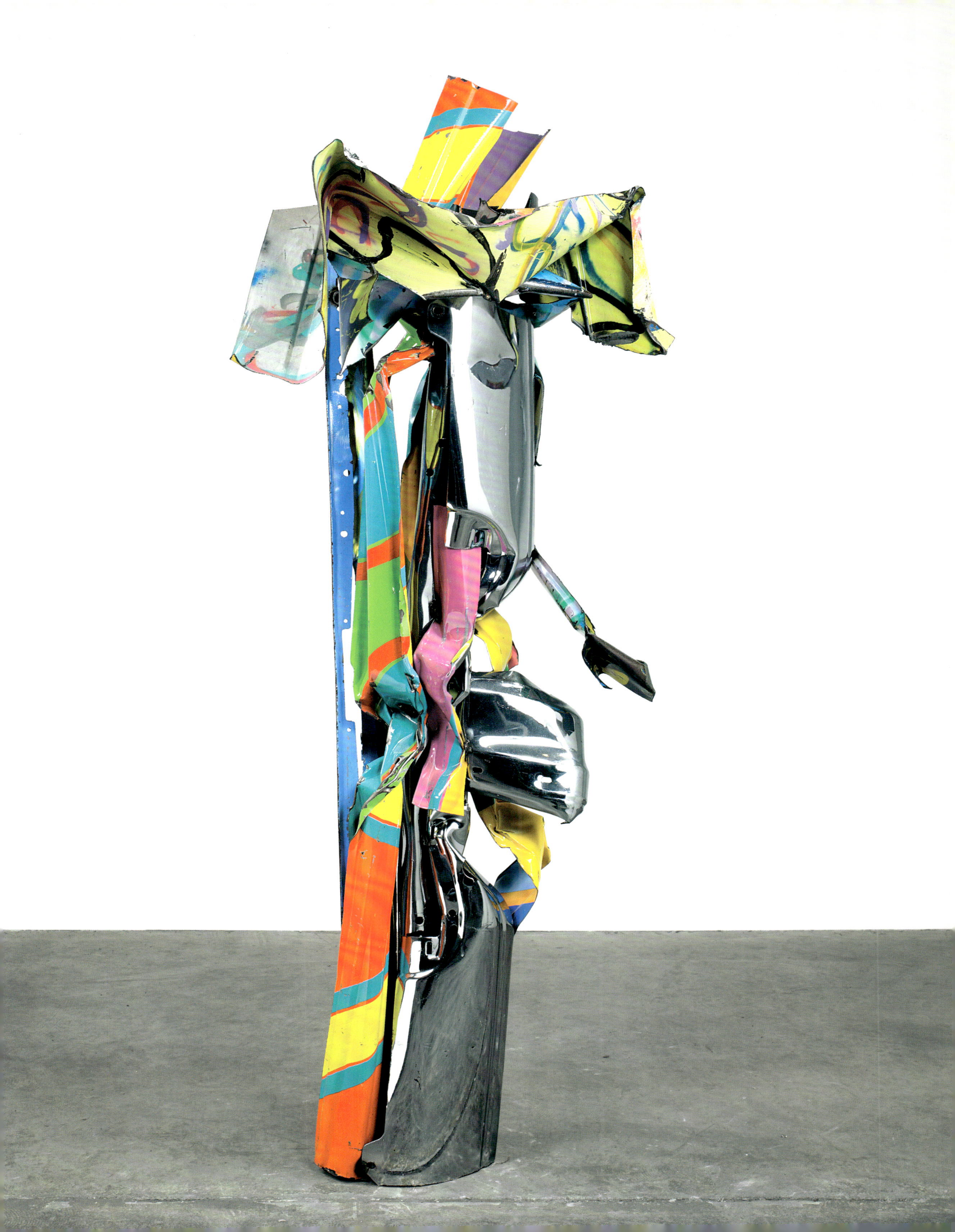

8. **Mr. Singing Boxer**, 2005

painted and chromed steel
75 x 26 x 22"

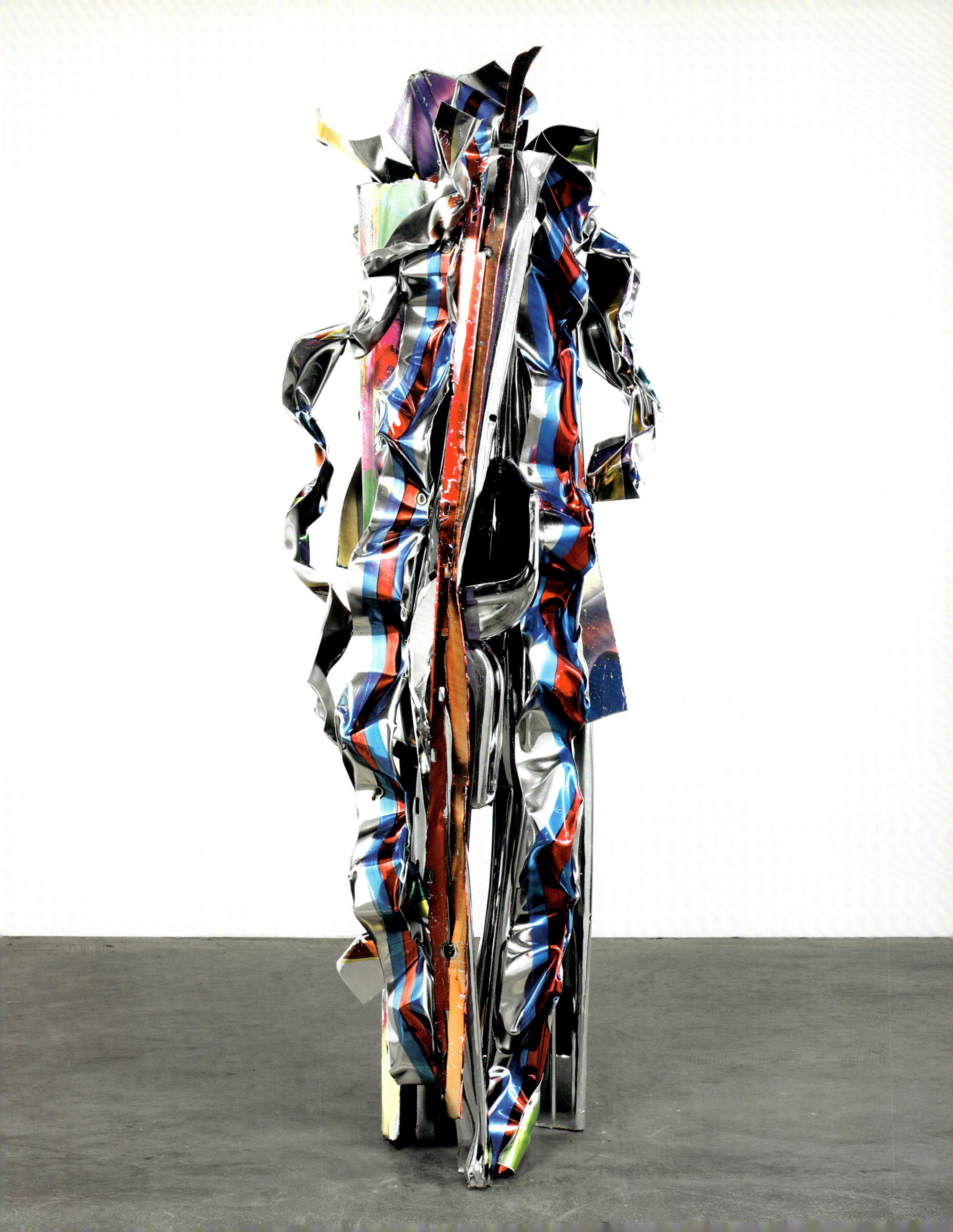

9. **Sphinx**, 2004

painted and chromed steel
103 x 57 x 56"

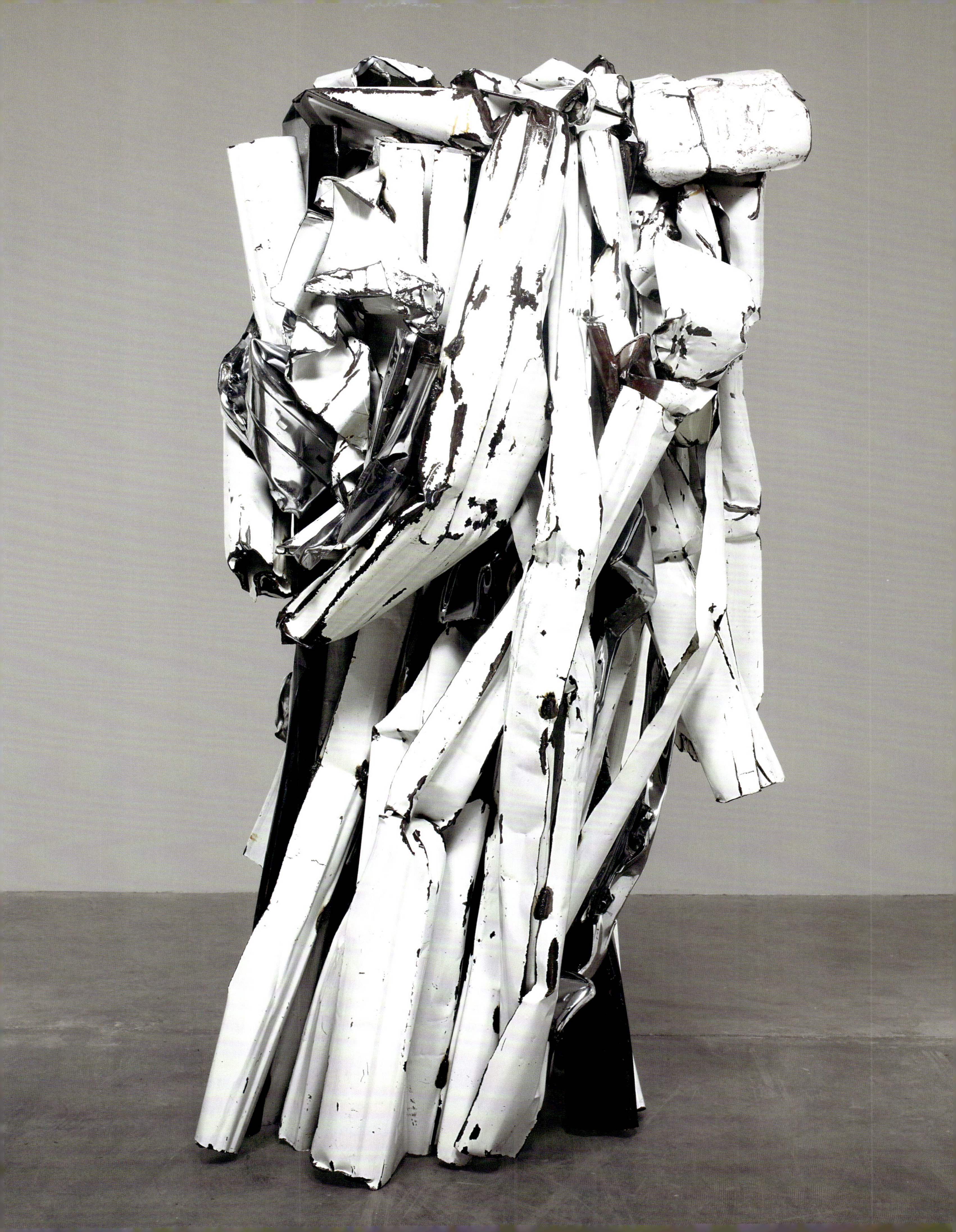

10. Wandering Gargoyle, 2005

painted and chromed steel
75 ½ x 62 x 65"

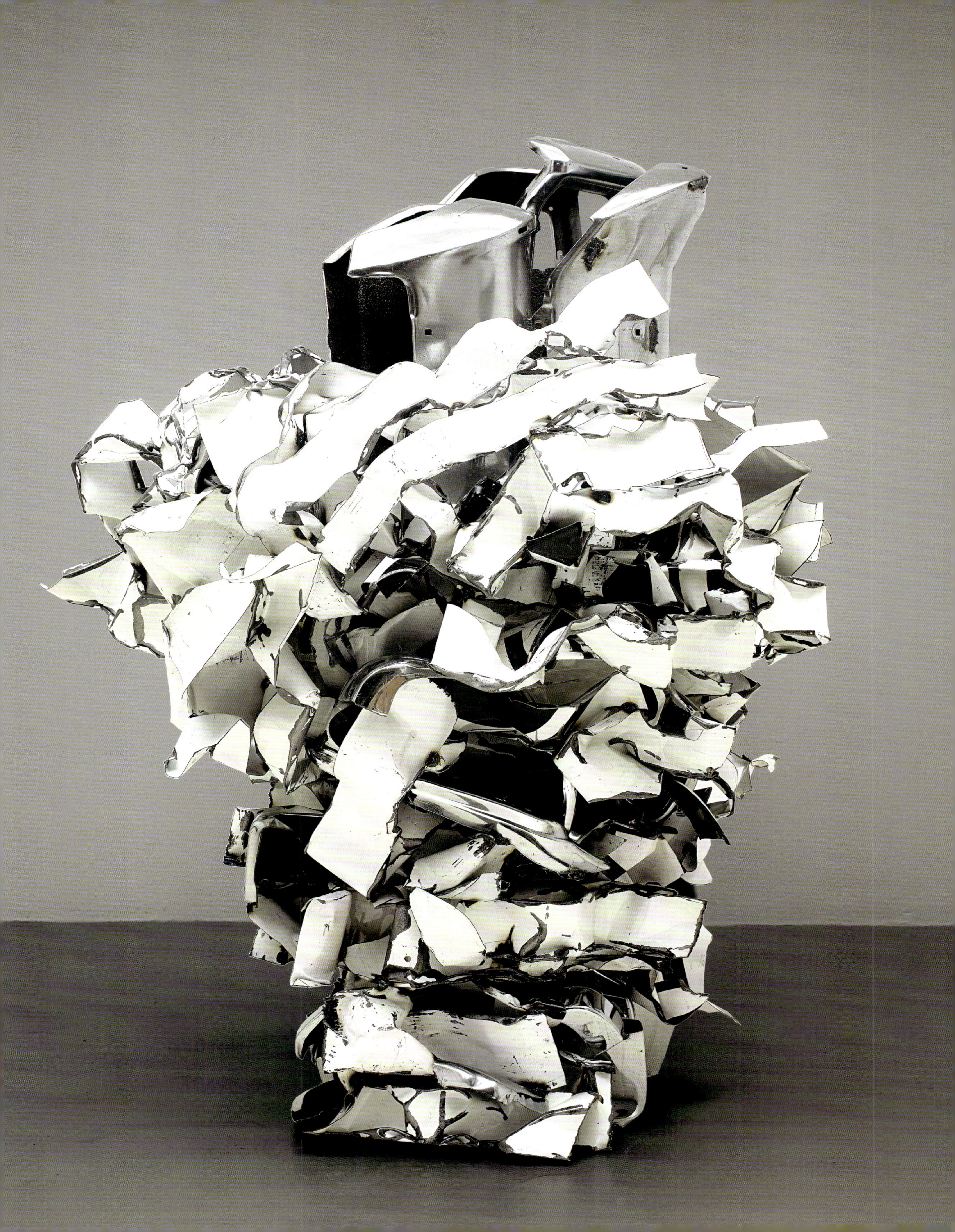

11. **Neptune's Cap**, 2005

painted and chromed steel
95 x 72 x 53"

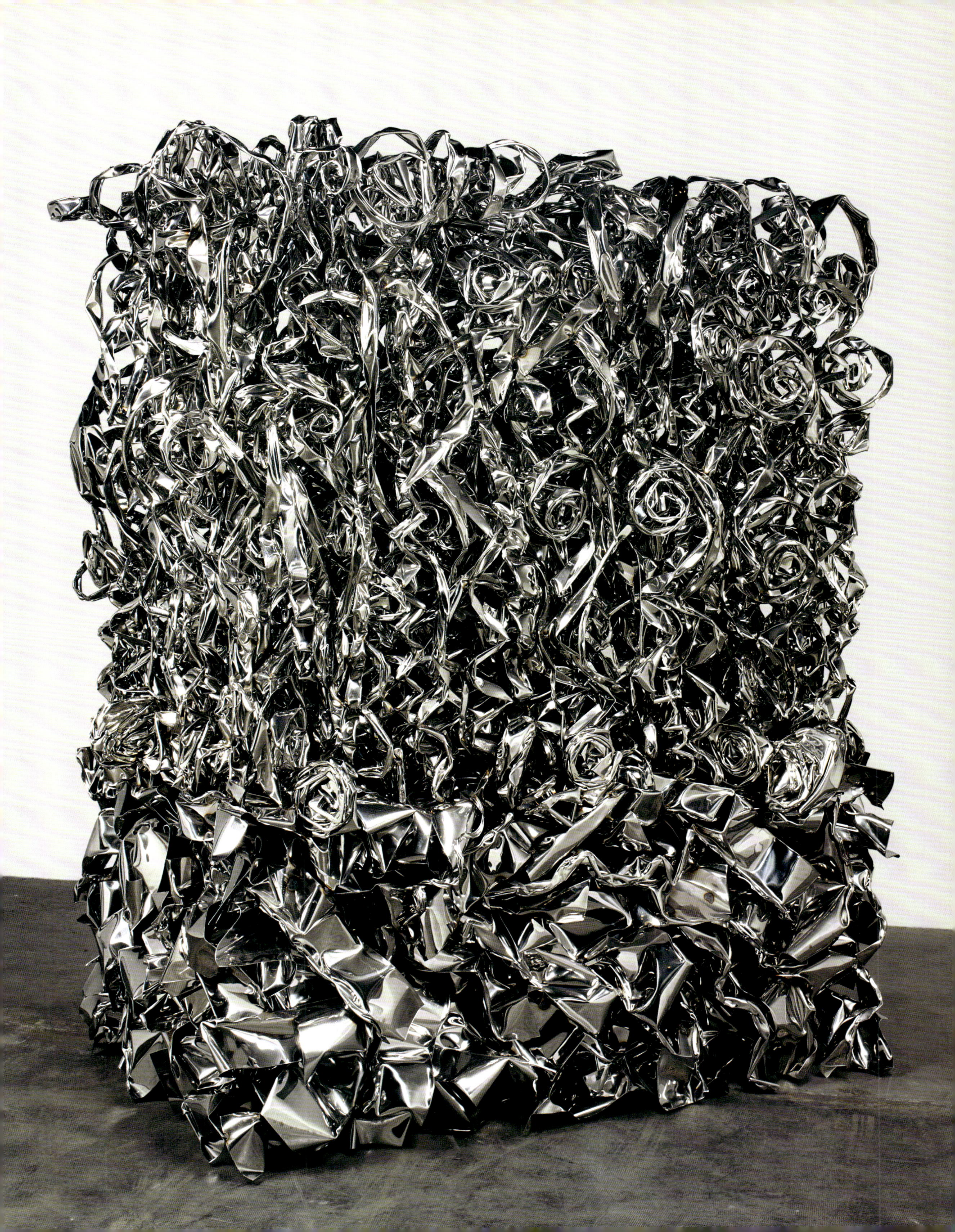

12. **Roots**, 2005

painted and chromed steel
72 x 36 x 36"

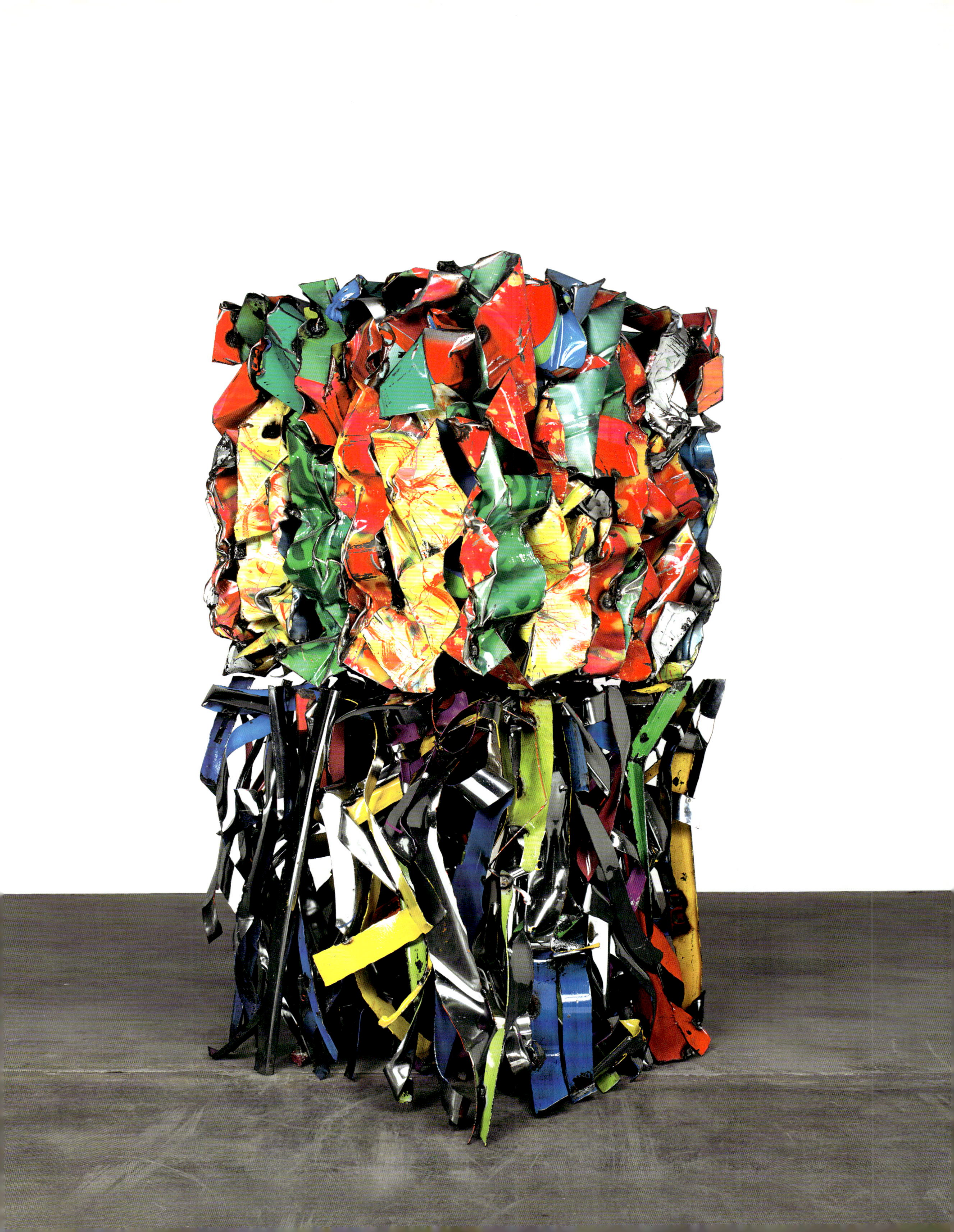

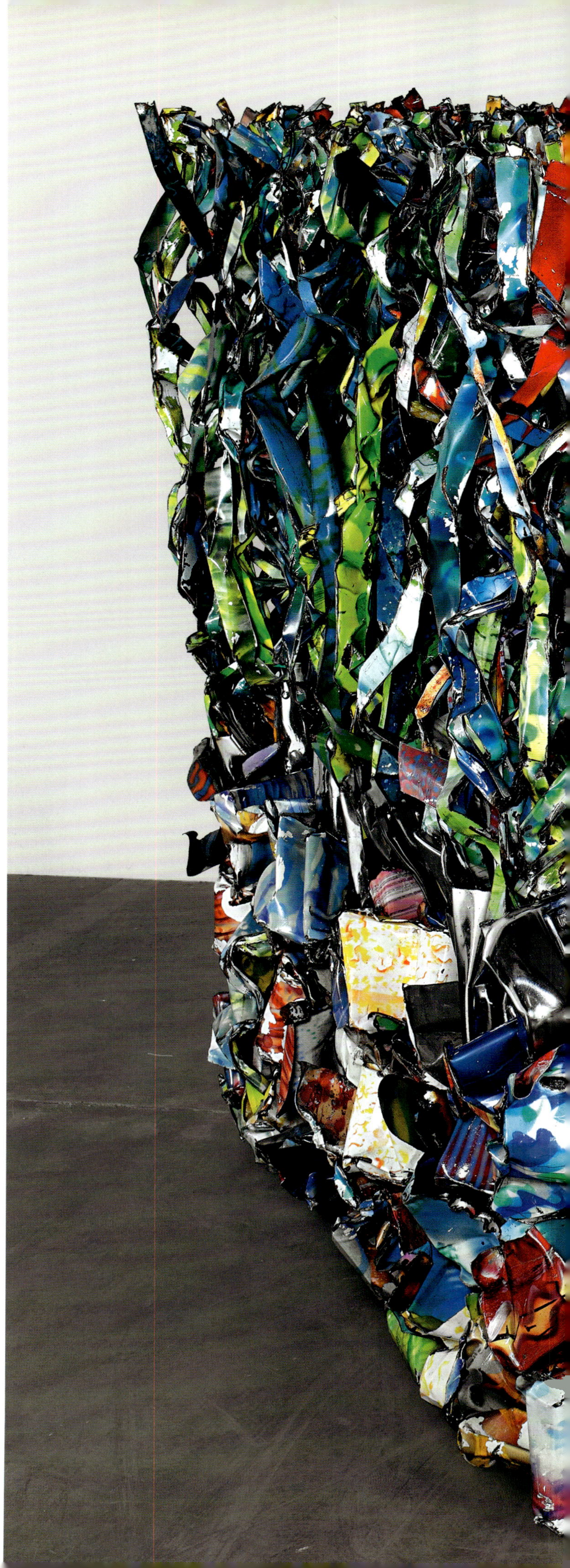

13. Thicket, 1997

painted and chromed steel
94 x 99 x 96"

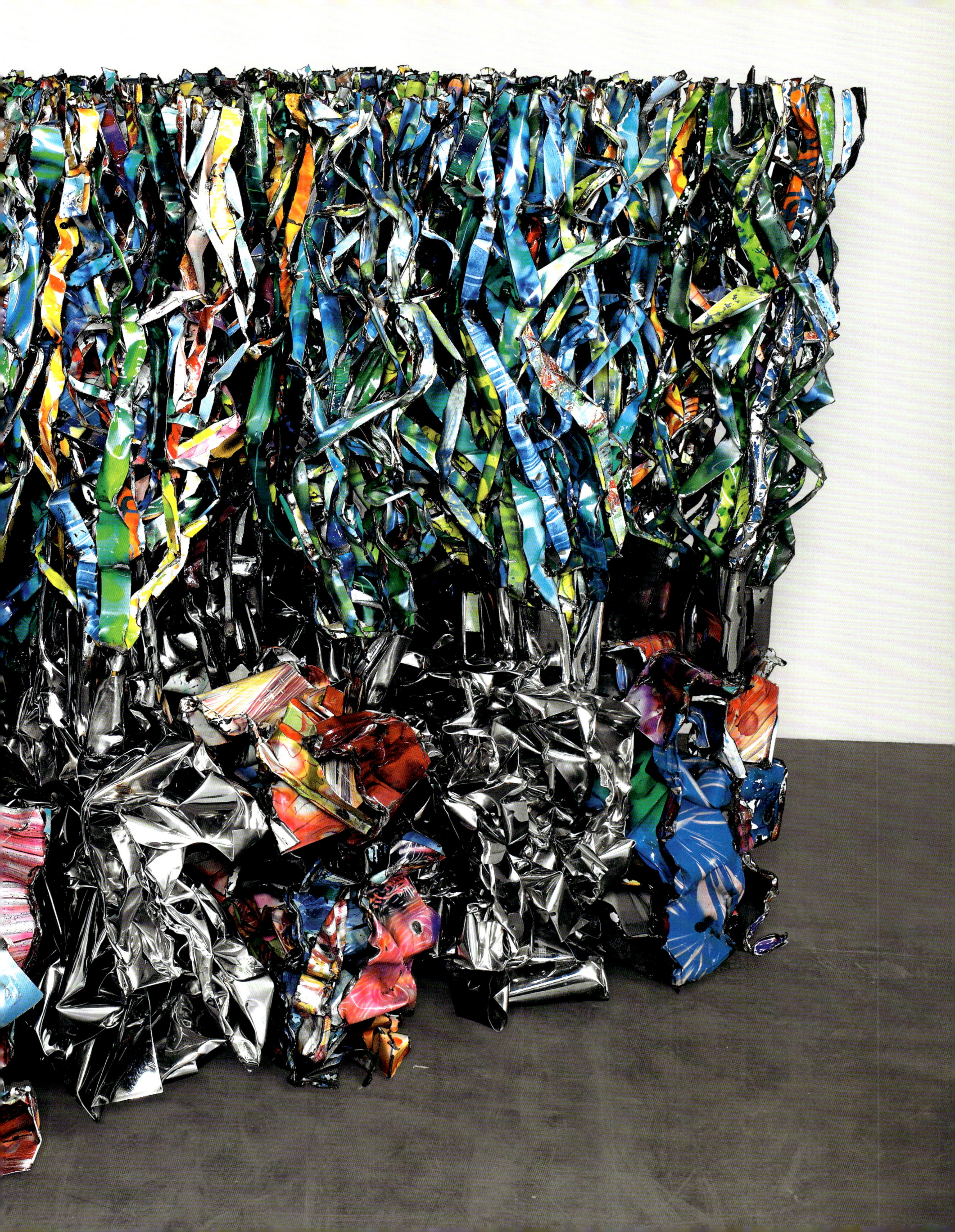

14. **Memo to Mozart**, 2005

painted and chromed steel
37 ½ x 34 x 18 ½"

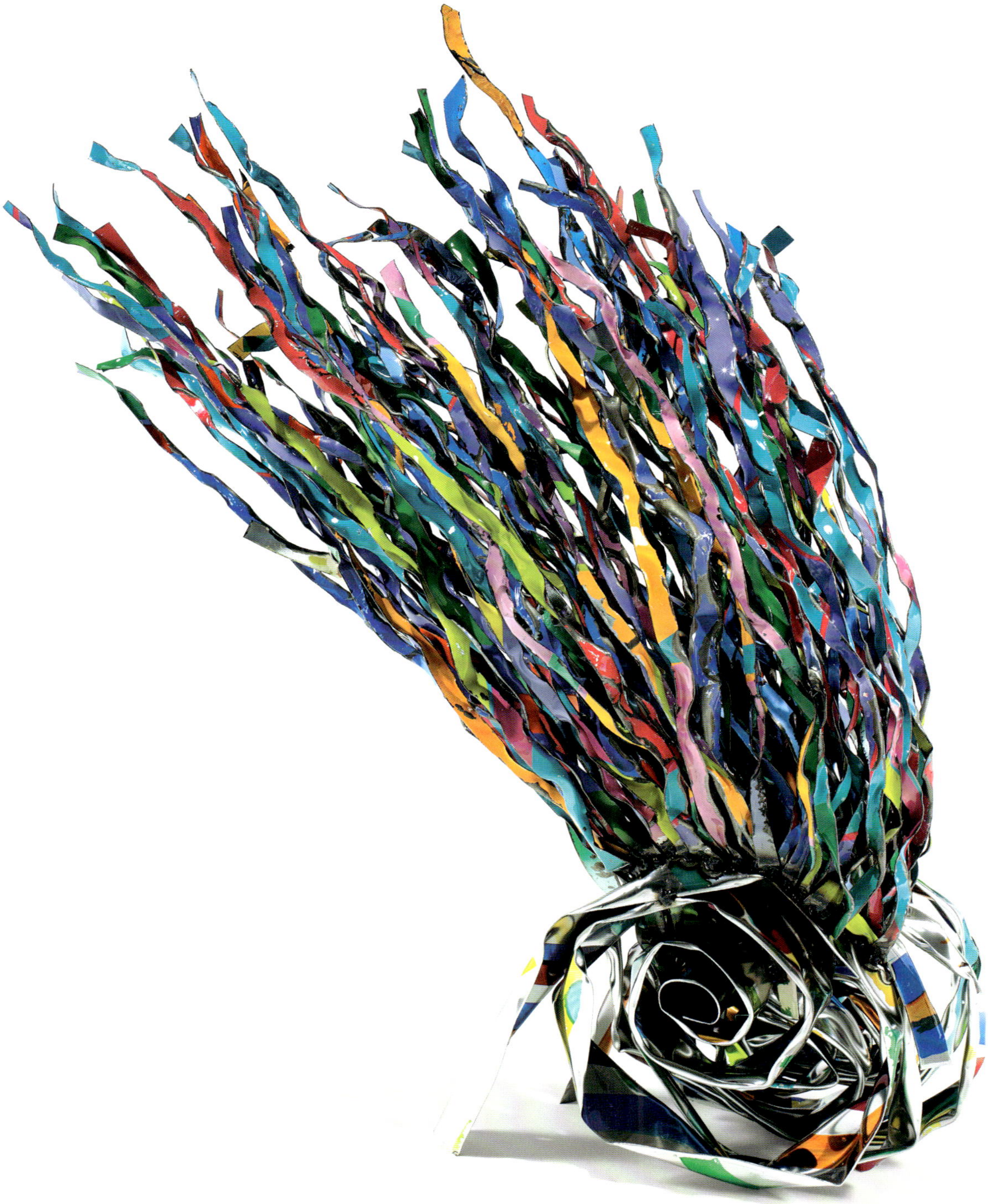

15. **Memo to Bach**, 2005

painted and chromed steel
36 x 26 ¼ x 18 ½"

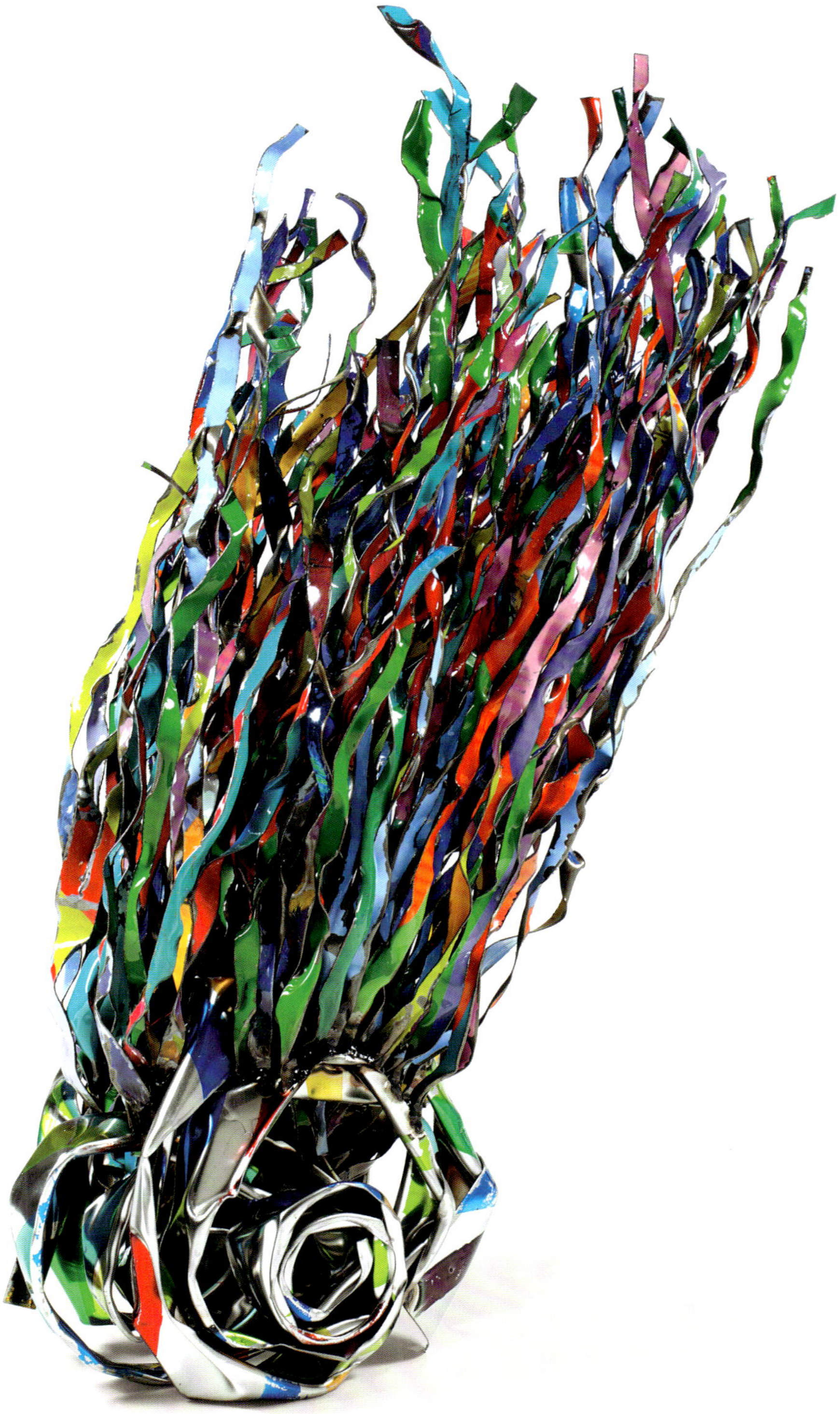

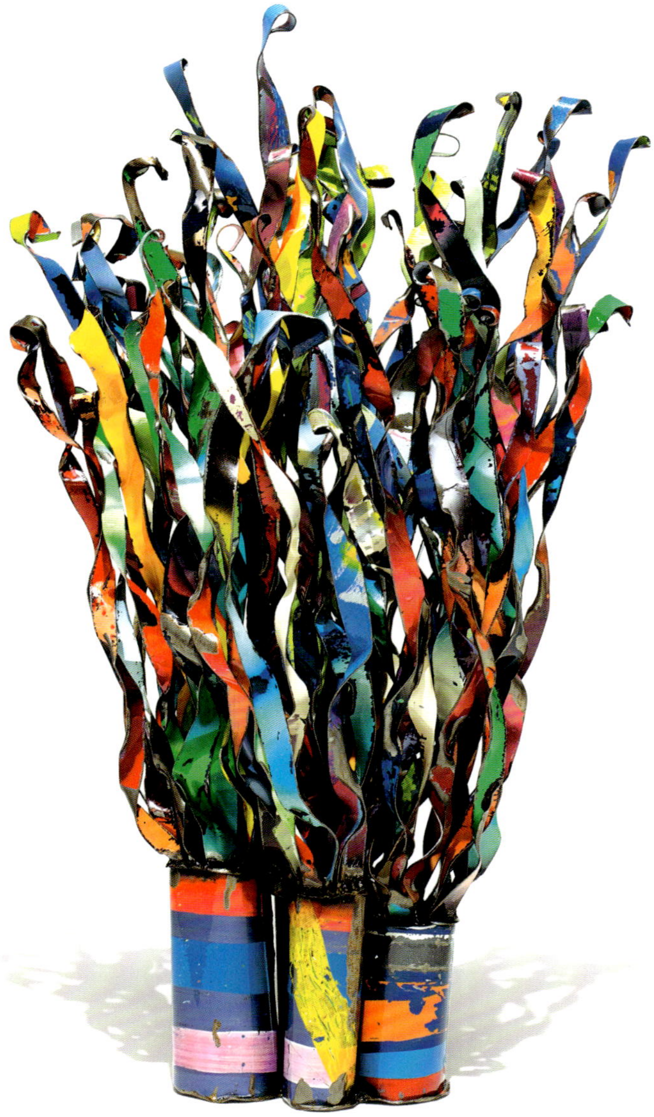

16. **Bluish Moon**, 2005

painted and chromed steel
28 5/8 x 17 x 15 3/8"

17. **Littlest Blue Moon**, 2005

painted and chromed steel
25 5/8 x 13 1/2 x 11 3/4"

18. **Blue Moonish**, 2005

painted and chromed steel
27 x 14 5/8 x 12 3/4"

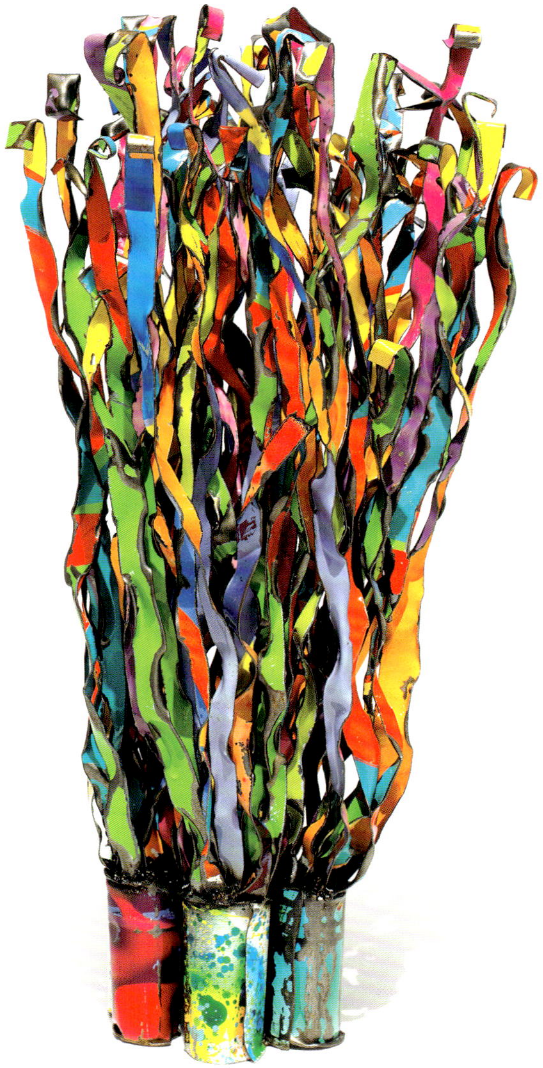

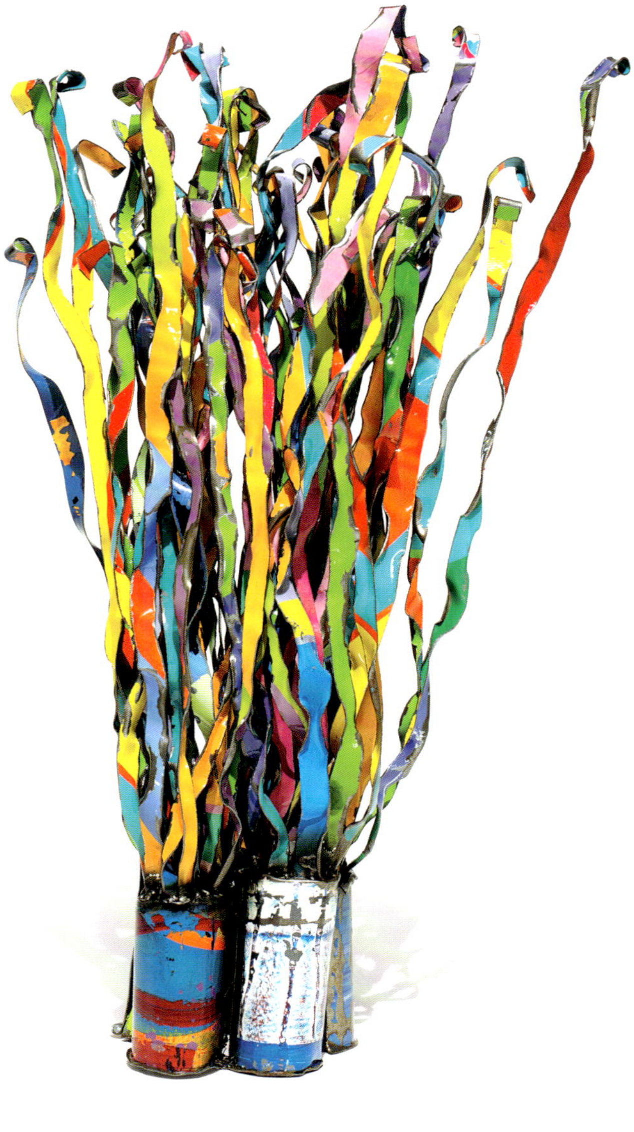

19. **Winner of 16 Diction Awards**, 2005

painted and chromed steel
29 x 31 x 24 ½"

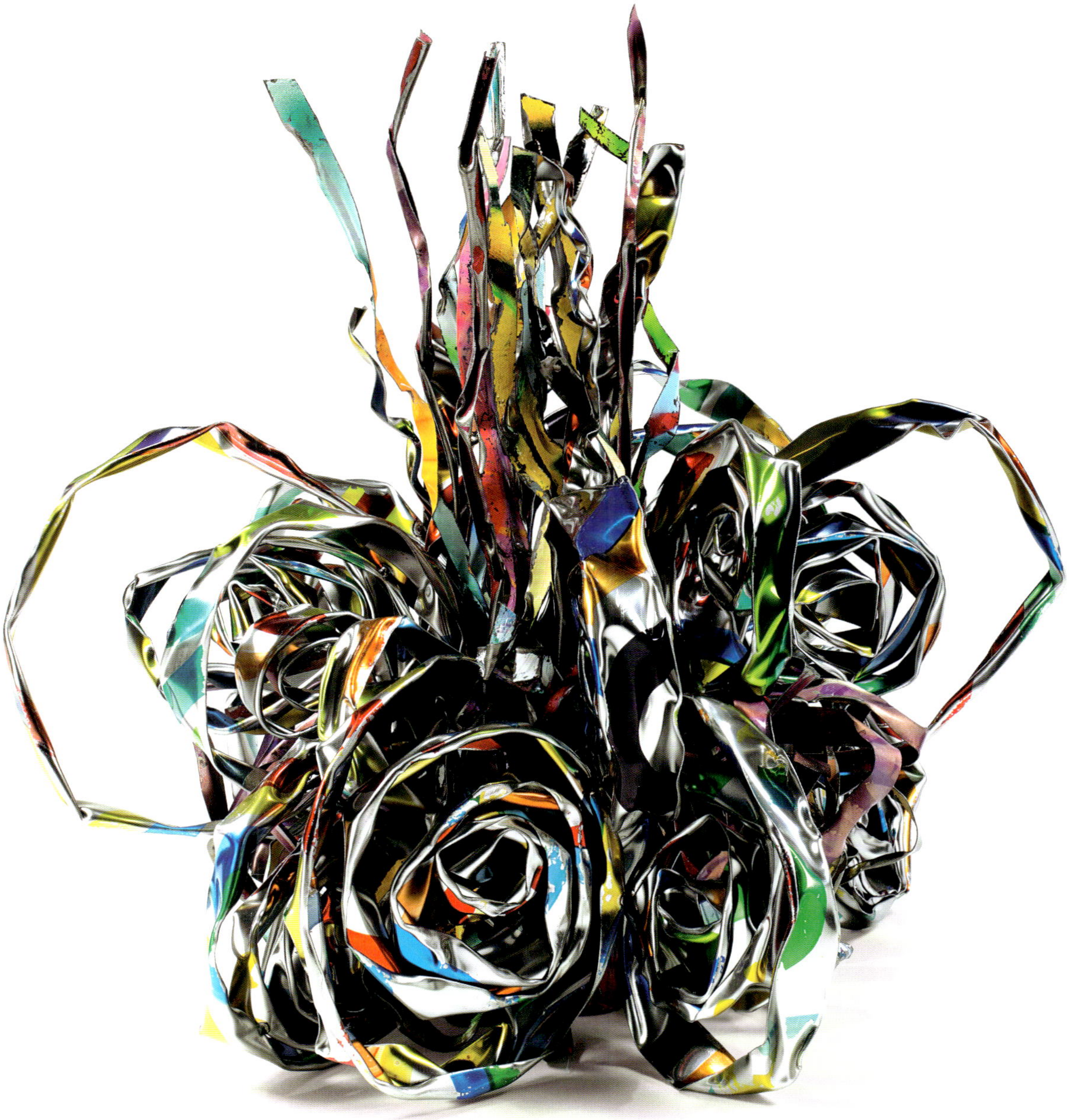

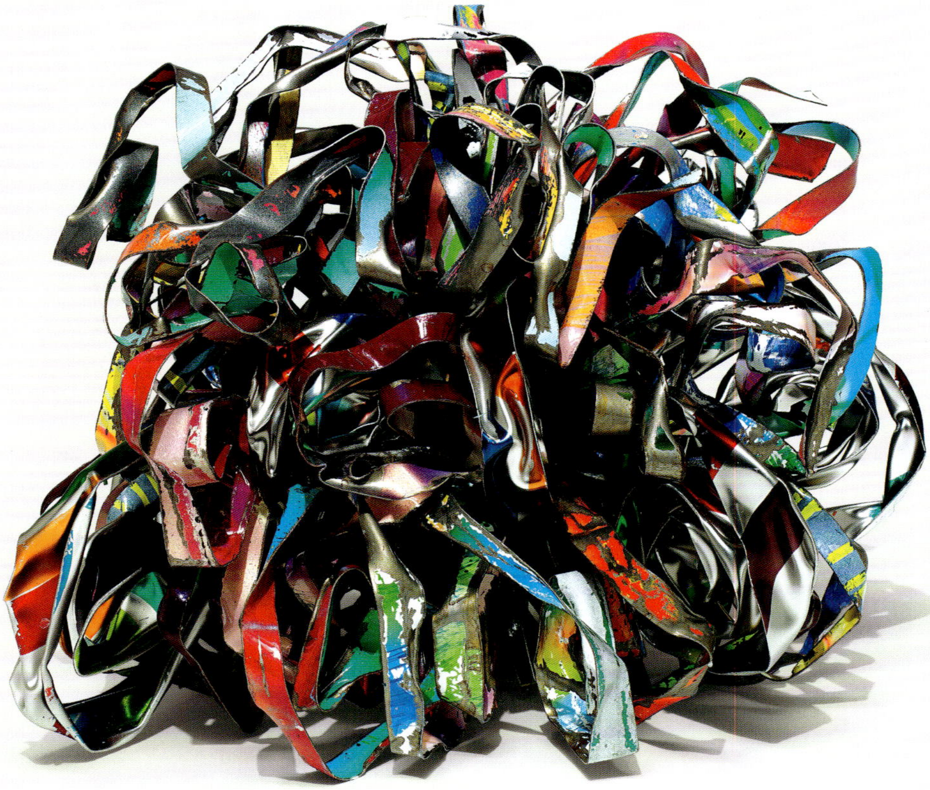

20. Zulu Igloo, 2005

painted and chromed steel
15 ¼ x 21 x 16 ½"

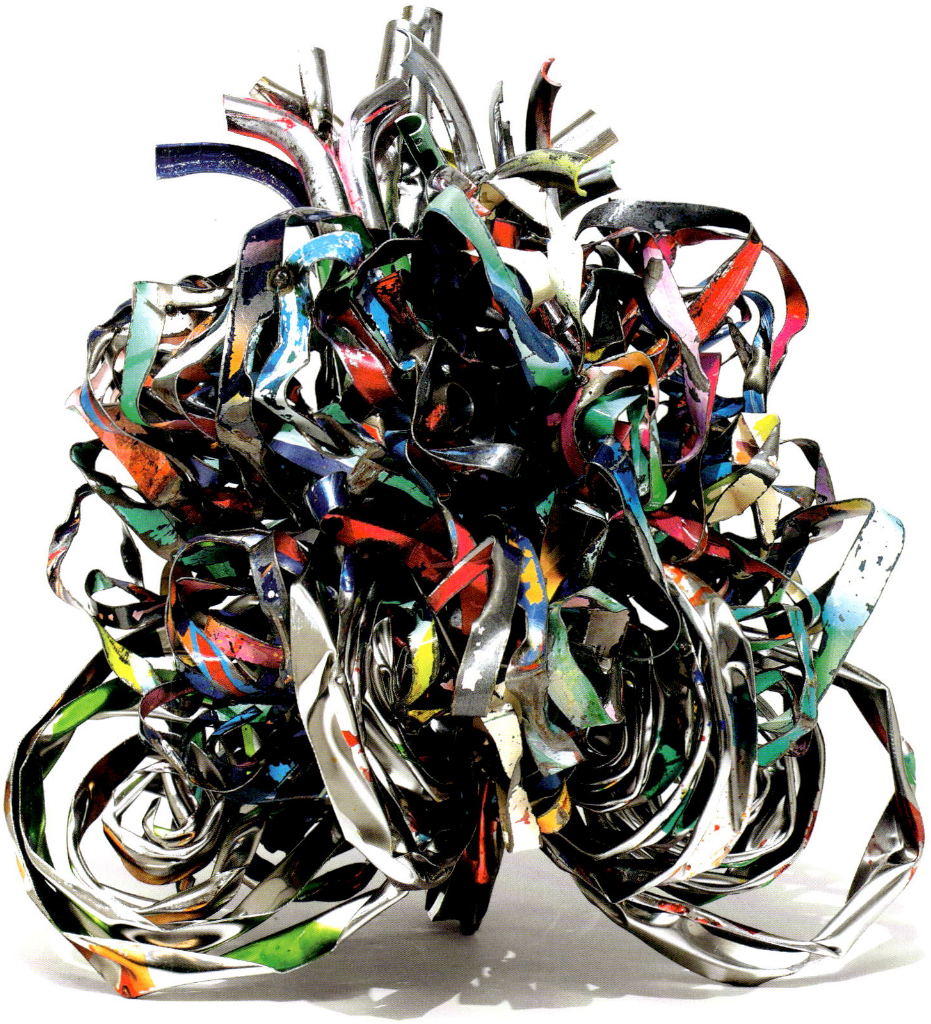

21. **You be Jekyll, I'll Hide**, 2005

painted and chromed steel
22 ½ x 19 ¾ x 18"

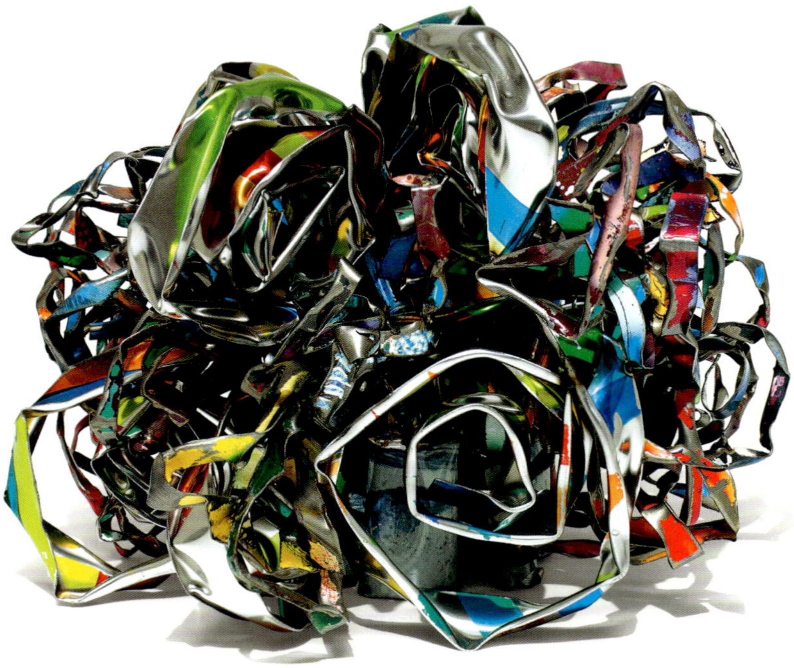

22. Three Yen & A Maybe, 2005

painted and chromed steel
15 x 21 ½ x 19 ½"

23. Pancake Pansy, 2005

painted and chromed steel
12 ½ x 18 ½ x 17 ½"

24. Pass the Breeze, 2005

painted and chromed steel
16 ½ x 21 x 19"

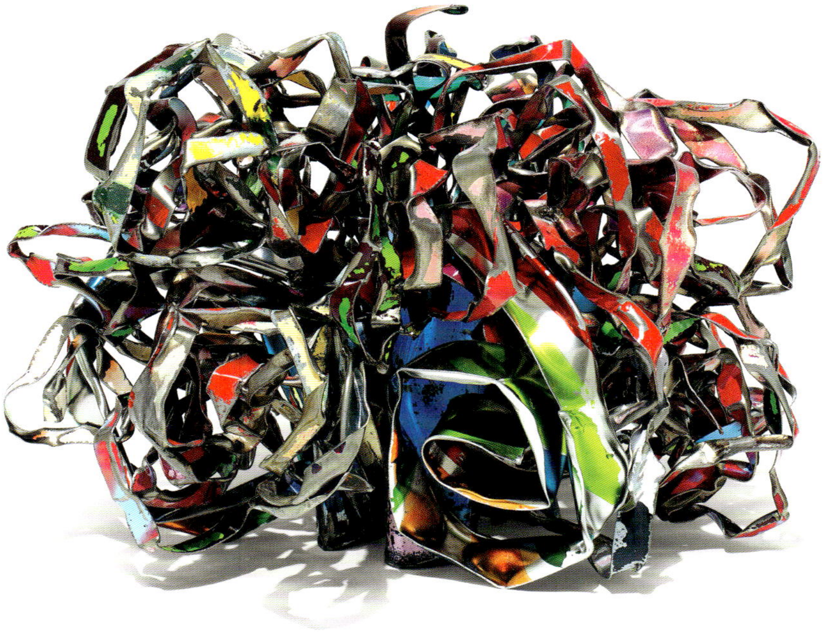

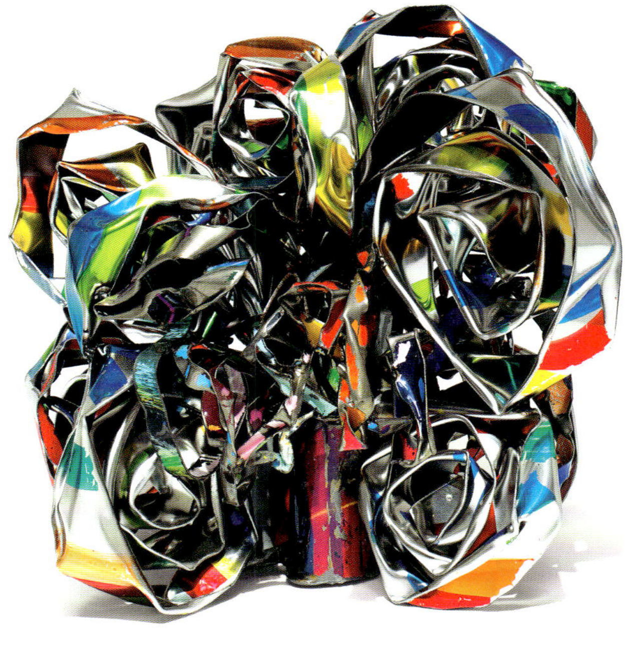

CHECK LIST

1. Mrs. Swayed Schwooz, 2005, painted and chromed steel, 84 ½ x 74 ¾ x 41"
2. Madam ZooZoo, 2005, painted and chromed steel, 80 x 25 x 22"
3. Mr. Mumblecrust, 2005, painted and chromed steel, 74 ½ x 44 x 39 ¼"
4. Rocket Ralph, 2005, painted and chromed steel, 75 x 26 x 22"
5. Ms. Trixie Friganza, 2005, painted and chromed steel, 76 x 32 ¾ x 23 ½"
6. SGT. Clappingstone, 2005, painted and chromed steel, 71 ½ x 26 x 23"
7. Wanda Wedgie, 2005, painted and chromed steel, 77 ¾ x 38 ½ x 27"
8. Mr. Singing Boxer, 2005, painted and chromed steel, 75 x 26 x 22"
9. Sphinx, 2004, painted and chromed steel, 103 x 57 x 56"
10. Wandering Gargoyle, 2005, painted and chromed steel, 75 ½ x 62 x 65"
11. Neptune's Cap, 2005, painted and chromed steel, 95 x 72 x 53"
12. Roots, 2005, painted and chromed steel, 72 x 36 x 36"
13. Thicket, 1997, painted and chromed steel, 94 x 99 x 96"
14. Memo to Mozart, 2005, painted and chromed steel, 37 ½ x 34 x 18 ½"
15. Memo to Bach, 2005, painted and chromed steel, 36 x 26 ¼ x 18 ½"
16. Bluish Moon, 2005, painted and chromed steel, 28 ⅝ x 17 x 15 ⅜"
17. Littlest Blue Moon, 2005, painted and chromed steel, 25 ⅝ x 13 ½ x 11 ¾"
18. Blue Moonish, 2005, painted and chromed steel, 27 x 14 ⅝ x 12 ¾"
19. Winner of 16 Diction Awards, 2005, painted and chromed steel, 29 x 31 x 24 ½"
20. Zulu Igloo, 2005, painted and chromed steel, 15 ¼ x 21 x 16 ½"
21. You be Jekyll, I'll Hide, 2005, painted and chromed steel, 22 ½ x 19 ¾ x 18"
22. Three Yen & A Maybe, 2005, painted and chromed steel, 15 x 21 ½ x 19 ½"
23. Pancake Pansy, 2005, painted and chromed steel, 12 ½ x 18 ½ x 17 ½"
24. Pass the Breeze, 2005, painted and chromed steel, 16 ½ x 21 x 19"

Cover: **Neptune's Cap**, 2005 (detail)

Photography: Ellen Labenski, Kerry Ryan McFate, Aram Jibilian

Design: Tomo Makiura

Production: Paul Pollard, Tucker Capparell

Color Correction: Motohiko Tokuta

Printing: Meridian Printing, East Greenwich, Rhode Island

ISBN: 1930743548